Messages from Heaven

To Help You

BE A
SHINING
STAR!

Second Edition

PAMELA JOY
Spreading Joy through God's Word

NIV: Scriptures taken from the Holy Bible, New International Version®, NIV®. Copyright © 1973, 1978, 1984, 2011 by Biblica, Inc.™ Used by permission of Zondervan. All rights reserved worldwide. www.zondervan.com The "NIV" and "New International Version" are trademarks registered in the United States Patent and Trademark Office by Biblica, Inc.™

WestBow Press books may be ordered through booksellers or by contacting:

WestBow Press
A Division of Thomas Nelson & Zondervan
1663 Liberty Drive
Bloomington, IN 47403
www.westbowpress.com
1 (866) 928-1240

ISBN: 978-1-9736-6029-3 (sc)
ISBN: 978-1-9736-6030-9 (e)

Library of Congress Control Number: 2019904473

Print information available on the last page.

WestBow Press rev. date: 07/09/2019

WESTBOW
P R E S S®
A DIVISION OF THOMAS NELSON
& ZONDERVAN

Dedication

SECOND EDITION

In loving memory of my parents,
Francine E. Koehler, who taught me to love God,
and
William F. Koehler, who taught me to love unconditionally

FIRST EDITION
In loving memory of my brother,
William Michael Koehler,
and
for his daughters,
Danielle Cristine and Nicole Annette

A Personal Note from the Author

Messages from Heaven was a huge undertaking for me. Overwhelming and frustrating at times, but always stimulating, inspiring, and fulfilling. It's true—God doesn't just use the best, brightest, and most successful individuals to accomplish His work on earth. He often uses average people, so the glory is His. To God be the glory—for without Him, this book would not be possible! So, as you learn and grow from the collection of messages presented in this book, I urge you to ask yourself...

What special things can I do for and with the Lord that are impossible without Him? Then, ask Him to work in and through you to accomplish those things–because nothing is impossible with God.

A Special Message to PARENTS

God has called you not only to teach the Word of God to your children but also to live His Word daily. May the Messages from Heaven, as written in the Bible and presented in this book, help you and your children to **BE SHINING STARS for God**, the Creator of heaven and earth.

These commandments that I give you today are to be on your hearts. Impress them on your children. Talk about them when you sit at home and when you walk along the road, when you lie down and when you get up. Tie them as symbols on your hands and bind them on your foreheads.
–Deuteronomy 6:6-8 (see also, 11:18-19)

Acknowledgments

First and foremost, I thank the Holy Spirit that lives within me for the opportunity to learn and grow while working on this project and for the inspiration, motivation, forbearance, and perseverance required to complete it.

A special thanks to those whose efforts have assisted in the preparation of this book:
Reverend Warren Reichert for his professional advisement and noteworthy comments.
Kristen Robinson for her suggestions and edits during the developmental stages of this project.
Stephanie Baker for implementing a homeschooling lesson plan to edit and review this book.
Christian Baker for his diligent study of this book and for his enthusiastic and encouraging response.
Nicole Naranjo for her pertinent perspective and valuable suggestions.
Kelsey Haugen for her expert editing and invaluable attention to detail.
Target age group participants Blayze Johnson, Lhyric Johnson, Caleb Lilje, Brynn Lilje, and Maria Naranjo for their time, enthusiasm, and favorable reviews.
Sharon Hartmann and Elissa Payne for their helpful comments during final revisions.

A personal thanks to:
Kevin S. West and his wife, Debby, for the inspiration to write this second edition.
George Prager and his wife, Vicki, who were earthly angels to my dad during his illness.
Dear friend, Mary Beth Butler for always being there to share in the ups and downs of life.
Godmother and loving Aunt, Barbara Kittner, for continuing where my mother left off in my life.
Aunts, Mary Goodenough, Laurel Gottardo, and Kathleen Considine, for extraordinarily blessed and loving kinships.

Most especially, I thank my esteemed husband James B. Dlugos for his love, support, encouragement, understanding, and patience all these years.

Part One

Introduction to The Written Word

All Scripture is God-breathed and is useful for teaching … –2 Timothy 3:16

IMPORTANT NOTE to READERS:

★   Answers to SHINING STARS statements are __underlined__ on each page.

***In the beginning God created the heavens and the earth.* –Genesis 1:1**

God created everything and everyone on purpose and for a purpose. That includes you and me! His specific plan for you is different from His plan for me. However, He's created us ALL to live and shine–for Him–through the unique and special gifts He's given us.

For you created my inmost being; you knit me together in my mother's womb. … all the days ordained for me were written in your book before one of them came to be. –Psalm 139:13,16

But, because God granted us the freedom of choice called freewill, not everyone chooses to follow Him or His plan. We are free to think, say, and do as we like. How we react or respond to things is our choice, and we make lots of choices every day! What kinds of choices have you made today?

Even when we commit to follow God and His perfect plan, no matter how hard we try, we sometimes fail and sin against Him by making poor choices. The Bible explains why we fail and has ALL the Messages from Heaven that we need to live faithfully and shine each day.

Direct my footsteps according to your word; let no sin rule over me. –Psalm 119:133

So, come along and have some fun as we learn more about God's Written Word, so you can BE A SHINING STAR here on God's earth!

Let's begin with the heavenly realms. While creating the various levels of heaven, God created a multitude of spirits we refer to as His heavenly hosts. He divided them into classes (groups) known as the angelic order and gave each one specific responsibilities. One class, called angels, cares for us here on earth. Their assignment is to guard and guide us. It's exciting to know they'll watch over us, help us to make loving choices, and lead us to God's truth, if we allow them.

For he will command his angels concerning you to guard you in all your ways … –Psalm 91:11

"See, I am sending an angel ahead of you to guard you along the way and to bring you to the place I have prepared. Pay attention to him and listen to what he says. Do not rebel against him …"
–Exodus 23:20-21

God created angel spirits to be stronger and more powerful than humans, but they are not God. They are His mighty servants—created to do specific tasks for Him in the heavens and on earth.

Praise the LORD, you his angels, you mighty ones who do his bidding*, who obey his word.
–Psalm 103:20 (see also, Psalm 103:21)

We are to respect the power and work of <u>God's angels</u>, but we are never to worship them. God is our Creator. We praise, worship, and pray to Him only as the Holy Trinity**.

Do you know who was corrected for worshiping one of God's angels? To find the answer, turn to Revelation 22:8-9 in your Bible.

Shining stars respect and listen to _ _ _'_ _ _ _ _ _ _ .

*telling, warning, directing
**Father, Son, and Holy Spirit

Unfortunately, not all angels can be called God's angels any longer. Shortly after God created the heavens, one of His brightest angels became prideful and rebellious. Wanting to rule rather than serve, this angel deceptively persuaded a large group of the angels to turn away from God and follow him instead. He then led them into a war against God's faithful angels. That angel, known as Satan or the devil, shines no more. He and his followers were defeated and forced to leave the heavenly realm, where God lives and reigns.

Then war broke out in heaven. Michael and his angels fought against the dragon, and the dragon and his angels fought back. But he was not strong enough, and they lost their place in heaven. The great dragon was hurled down—that ancient serpent called the devil, or Satan, who leads the whole world astray. He was hurled to the earth, and his angels with him. –Revelation 12:7-9

Just as Satan persuaded the fallen angels to follow him instead of God, he quickly tricked mankind into disobeying God, too. Now, we live in a sinful world.

… the devil, … he is a liar and the father of lies. –John 8:44

Satan and his army continue to fight against God and His goodness by attacking us here on earth. Yes, we're all caught in a spiritual war of good versus evil. However, God has already defeated Satan–God wins in the end! So, if we reject the devil and choose to accept, follow, and serve God, we can join Him in victory and become the shining stars that He created us to be.

*Dear children, do not let anyone lead you astray. The one who does what is right is righteous … The one who does what is sinful is of the devil, because the devil has been sinning from the beginning. …
–1 John 3:7-8*

Therefore, we must watch out! Satan and his army are continually at work trying to cloud our thoughts and good judgment. They want to keep us from seeing, feeling, and following God's perfect, loving light.

Evil forces are attempting to:
- CONFUSE us by making bad choices look fun and exciting, so we'll choose wrong over right.
- DELAY us by leading us away from our goals so that we don't reach them.
- DISCOURAGE us by making us look at our problems rather than our blessings.
- FRUSTRATE us by making us feel defeated and unwilling to try because we think we'll fail.
- TEMPT us by encouraging us to do something wrong to get what we want.
- MOCK us by luring others to make fun of or criticize us for our faith.
- TRICK us by twisting the truth so we think we are doing the right thing when it really isn't.

Have you ever…
-been afraid to try something new?
-said, "I'll do it later," but later never came?
-wanted to hurt someone for hurting you?
-wanted something so badly that you lied, cheated, or stole to get it?
-done something wrong just to be accepted or liked by someone?
-made fun of or said unkind things to or about someone?

If you said yes to any of the above, you've been deceived by the evil one and his army. If we aren't careful, they will lead us in the wrong direction–away from God and His perfect plan for us. Then, good choices become very difficult to make.

For our struggle is … against the spiritual forces of evil in the heavenly realms*. –Ephesians 6:12

Be alert … Your enemy the devil prowls around like a roaring lion looking for someone to devour. Resist him, standing firm in the faith… –1 Peter 5:8

*The earth's heavenly atmosphere—not God's Heavenly Realm, which is much higher.

Studying the Bible helps us to recognize clouded and deceptive thoughts so that we can see God's <u>truth</u> more clearly. The <u>Bible</u> teaches us how to use His <u>Word</u> as a powerful weapon to fight and overcome evil influences, so we can shine our brightest!

> *Finally, be strong in the Lord and in his mighty power. Put on the full armor of God, so that you can take your stand against the devil's schemes. ... Take the helmet of salvation and the sword of the Spirit, which is the word of God.* –Ephesians 6:10-11, 17

We'll have fun learning more about the full armor of God in Part Three—the activities section.

Shining stars read the Bible daily and ask the Holy Spirit for understanding. They dig deep into the Word so that it will take root in their hearts. As God's Word grows in our hearts, our lives become fruitful. We'll learn more about the Holy Spirit and fruitfulness in Part Two. So, let's read on! Heavenly angels are leading us to powerful messages found in the Holy Bible.

> *All your words are true; all your righteous laws are eternal*.* –Psalm 119:160

> *Show me your ways, LORD, teach me your paths. Guide me in your truth and teach me ...* –Psalm 25:4-5

Shining stars live by God's _ _ _ _ _, which is His _ _ _ _ found in the _ _ _ _ _!

*endless, forever

The Bible doesn't tell us what angels look like nor does it tell us their names except for a few, like Gabriel and Michael. It does, however, tell us that God sends heavenly angels to guard and guide us in many ways. Unlike fallen angels, heavenly angels lead us to good, positive thoughts. Negative, depressing, or hopeless thoughts are never from God's angels.

We can't see our thoughts; they are invisible. Angels, like thoughts, are also invisible. Only when it's essential (necessary) will God allow someone to see an angel. The Bible describes two ways in which His angels have appeared: to look like a person or as a vision in a dream.

Let's read about several angelic appearances recorded in the Bible. Look up the following Scriptures, and note which angels appeared physically as people and which appeared as visions in dreams.

Matthew 1:18-20, 2:13, 2:19-20
Luke 1:26-35, 2:9-15
Acts 5:18-19, 12:7-9, 16:9-10

Although most of us will never see an angel, they reach us in many ways. They whisper to us through our thoughts. They touch us by helping us to feel safe. They warn us of danger by sending us uneasy or odd feelings.

Can you think of a time when an angel may have spoken to you? Did you listen?

When we receive messages or help from one of God's angels, it's always for the good of all concerned. This means a heavenly angel would never hurt another one of God's children to help us. His angels must do what is best for everyone. God instructs angels to guide us in good, positive ways that please Him.

Angels are not here to shower us with material wealth (toys, gifts, or money). Instead, they help us create goodness and joy from the gifts God has given us. God has blessed each of us with special <u>talents</u> and spiritual <u>gifts</u> so that we can shine and contribute in our own individual ways. He asks us not to compare ourselves to others but to appreciate and use the gifts we have been given to help others.

... each of you has your own gift from God; one has this gift, another has that. –1 Corinthians 7:7

Every good and perfect gift is from above, coming down from the Father of the heavenly lights ...
–James 1:17

Shining stars are grateful for their own _ _ _ _ _ _ _ and _ _ _ _ _ !

Even though it's a choice, God expects us to use the gifts He's given us to do good, righteous things and <u>help</u> <u>others</u>. His Will (plan) is perfect, and He accomplishes great things through us when we choose to follow Him and use our gifts for His purpose.

"For I know the plans I have for you," declares the LORD, "plans to prosper you and not to harm you, plans to give you hope and a future." –Jeremiah 29:11

For we are God's handiwork, created in Christ Jesus to do good works, which God prepared in advance for us to do. –Ephesians 2:10

Each of you should use whatever gift you have received to serve others, as faithful stewards of God's grace in its various forms. –1 Peter 4:10

Do you know what your spiritual gifts are? If not, answering the following questions may help you identify them.

- What is one of your favorite things to do?
- What makes you happy?
- What do you do well?
- What do others say you do well?
- What is easy for you to do that others find hard to do?
- What do you dream about doing someday?
- How can you help others while doing these things?

Shining stars choose to use God's gifts to _ _ _ _ _ _ _ _ _ _!

It is also very important to <u>pray</u> (talk) to God <u>every</u> <u>day</u>. There is no set time or place to pray. We can pray to start the day and during play, before we sleep and when we weep.

The purposes of prayer are to:
PRAISE- "Wow! You are awesome, great, and mighty."
REPENT- "Oops! I'm sorry. I was wrong, and I want to make the right choice next time."
ASK- "Help! Please lead, guide, show, teach, and assist me."
YIELD- "Yes! I accept Your assistance and thank You for it."

Circle which part of PRAY each Bible Scripture below expresses.

If we confess our sins, he … will forgive us our sins … –1 John 1:9 **P R A Y**

Say to God, "How awesome are your deeds! …" –Psalm 66:3 **P R A Y**

Then you will call, and the LORD will answer; you will cry for help, and he will say: Here am I.
–Isaiah 58:9 **P R A Y**

… always giving thanks to God the Father for everything, in the name of our Lord Jesus Christ.
–Ephesians 5:20 **P R A Y**

FOR 	**always pray:**	
	∼ for GOD'S WILL:	1 John 5:14
	∼ in JESUS' NAME:	John 16:23
	∼ with FAITH/BELIEF:	Matthew 21:22

Shining stars _ _ _ _   _ _ _ _ _   _ _ _.

At times, we may think that God isn't listening to our prayers. This isn't true. He waits for the right time to answer us. We must be patient and trust that things will work out in God's <u>perfect timing</u>, not ours. And, sometimes, what we pray for isn't what is best for us. God often answers us in ways we haven't thought of, so we must look for other possible answers. Remember: we must seek <u>God's</u> <u>Will</u>, not our own. The closer and more faithful we are to God, the more likely our prayers will be in line with His plan for us.

I desire to do your will, my God; your law is within my heart. –Psalm 40:8

Then you will call on me and come and pray to me, and I will listen to you. –Jeremiah 29:12

Additional readings: Psalms 17:6, 33:20, 40:1, 66:19-20; John 15:7

Shining stars trust God's _ _ _ _ _ _ _ _ _ _ _ _ _ and believe _ _ _' _ _ _ _ is best!

Angel spirits were created by God to protect us and bring His messages to us, but it is God Himself in the form of the Holy Spirit that brings understanding. In the next section, symbolic angels will share important messages from heaven with you. These angels only symbolize (represent) God's messengers. We don't know their true identities or how they really look. The biblical messages they bring, however, are true. So, read on and pay close attention. God's messengers are joyfully leading you to His Word.

Now, turn the page and get ready for the HOLY SPIRIT to help you learn and understand these important messages so that you can become the shining star God created you to be!

Jesus said:
But the Advocate*, the Holy Spirit, whom the Father will send in my name, will teach you all things and will remind you of everything I have said to you. –John 14:26

*helper, supporter

Part Two

Messages for God's Children

Yet to all who did receive him, to those who believed in his name, he gave the right to become children of God. –John 1:12

We've learned that it's impossible to obey God on our own because evil entered the world when Satan turned against God and fell from heaven. That's when Satan came to earth and tricked mankind into disobeying God. Now we're all born into a sinful world, with sinful desires.

The good news is that God has graciously provided a way for us to be forgiven of our sins so that we can shine for Him and be all that He created us to be! How? Through His Son, Jesus Christ, who lived a perfect life, was unjustly crucified, died, and was resurrected (raised from the dead) to save us through Salvation. We'll read more about Salvation on page 25.

When we choose to accept Jesus as our Savior and turn our lives over to HIM, we are forgiven of our sins and given a new, spiritual way to live our lives with a helper, the Holy Spirit.

> …*"Repent and be baptized, every one of you, in the name of Jesus Christ for the forgiveness of your sins. And you will receive the gift of the Holy Spirit.* –Acts 2:38

Just like a flashlight can't shine without a power source, such as a battery, we can't shine for God and do the things He created for us to do without <u>the</u> <u>Holy</u> <u>Spirit</u>. He is the power source that lives within us. He works in Christians to help them become more like Christ. When we ask, listen, and follow the Spirit within, He'll guide us, direct us, and keep us from making bad and sinful decisions in life. Isn't it exciting to know we have a <u>supernatural</u> way to overcome sin and shine our brightest for God?!

> *But you will receive power when the Holy Spirit comes on you …* –Acts 1:8

Additional reading: 1 Corinthians 2:12-13

Shining stars trust the _ _ _ _ _ _ _ _ _ _ _ POWER of _ _ _   _ _ _ _   _ _ _ _ _ _ .

Jesus replied, "Very truly I tell you, no one can see the kingdom of God unless they are born again."
–John 3:3

You may be asking what Jesus meant by being "born again." Because we're born of earthly parents, we're all born with sinful desires of the flesh. But, if we choose to die to those worldly desires and ask Jesus into our hearts, we are born into a new life, a new way of living in the SPIRIT!

But now, by dying to what once bound us, we have been released from the law so that we serve in the new way of the Spirit, and not in the old way of the written code. –Romans 7:6

As our commitment to and understanding of God's Word takes root in our hearts and minds, the seeds of His Spiritual Fruit (planted in us when we turn our lives over to Jesus) will grow.

But the fruit of the spirit is love, joy, peace, forbearance*, kindness, goodness, faithfulness, gentleness, and self-control. … –Galatians 5:22-23

The Holy Spirit <u>helps</u> us to <u>grow</u> in our <u>fruit</u> so that we can live fruitful lives and shine brightly for God. We'll have fun with the Holy Spirit and Spiritual Fruit puzzle activities in Part Three.

The Holy Spirit _ _ _ _ _ shining stars to _ _ _ _ in spiritual _ _ _ _ _ !

*patience

Do you know why the Holy Spirit is symbolized as a white dove? To find the answer, turn to Matthew 3:16 in your Bible.

Additional readings: Mark 1:10; Luke 3:22; John 1:3

LOVE

Love is God's perfect light, which shines for eternity!

…Live as children of light (for the fruit of the light consists in all goodness, righteousness and truth) and find out what pleases the Lord. –Ephesians 5:8-10

God's children are filled with His love and light. As His children, we're commanded to walk in LOVE so that others may see, feel, experience, and accept God's love through our adages (words), attitudes, and actions.

And this is love: that we walk in obedience to his commands. … his command is that you walk in love. –2 John 1:6

Even though we know we are to respond lovingly to others, sometimes a negative emotion like anger or frustration becomes so strong that it clouds the loving light of God inside us. God understands and will help us to SAIL through our clouded thinking. ASK and LISTEN!

When you are overcome by a dark and unloving emotion, choose to **SAIL** through it!

Stop! Be still and silent as you breathe deeply.
Ask God and the Holy Spirit to shine supernatural light and love upon you.
Imagine His loving light bursting through your dark emotional cloud.
Let your light shine! Light lives with loving acts.

Additional readings: John 15:12; 1 John 4:7

What is Love?

Love is patient, love is kind. It does not envy, it does not boast, it is not proud. It does not dishonor others, it is not self-seeking, it is not easily angered, it keeps no record of wrongs. –1 Corinthians 13:4-5

Has someone ever:

-Made you feel worthless or stupid?

-Hurt or upset you?

-Criticized you?

-Made you feel special?

-Helped or encouraged you?

-Complimented you?

- How did each situation make you feel?
- How did you react/respond to the people in each situation?

God asks us to behave lovingly to everyone at all times, regardless of how they treat us.

"… Love your enemies, do good to those who hate you, bless those who curse you, pray for those who mistreat you. –Luke 6:27-28

Do not repay evil with evil or insult with insult. On the contrary, repay evil with blessing … –1 Peter 3:9

Do not say, "I'll do to them as they have done to me; I'll pay them back for what they did." –Proverbs 24:29

We've been instructed to live by the Golden Rule found in Matthew 7:12 and Luke 6:31:
DO TO OTHERS AS YOU WOULD HAVE THEM DO TO YOU.

- Would you want someone to gossip and say bad, untrue things about you?
- Would you want someone to make fun of or bully you?
- Would you want someone to lie to you?
- Would you want someone to cheat or steal from you?
- Would you want someone to keep reminding you of things you've done wrong?

Next time you get the urge to mistreat someone, remember: that urge comes from the forces of evil, not from God.

Shining stars live by the _ _ _ _ _ _   _ _ _ _!

JOY

You make known to me the path of life; you will fill me with joy in your presence ... –Psalm 16:11

The LORD has done great things for us, and we are filled with joy. –Psalm 126:3

People and things can make us happy for a while, but they don't fill us with joy. Joy comes from staying connected to our Creator. It's those who trust in God's love and His Word that are filled with joy. They know His will is best for them, and they choose to trust rather than worry too much. Joyous people look for God's goodness in everything. They focus on the good things in life, not the bad. They tend to think kind, loving thoughts. They strive to say and do nice things that please God. They gladly obey His Word without complaining.

Do everything without grumbling or arguing ... –Philippians 2:14

Do you want to be more joyful? Then, don't be a fault finder. Strive to see things through loving, not judgmental, eyes. Everything and everyone has good qualities—look for them!

Listening to worship music and singing songs of praise also bring us a joyful heart. It pleases God, too! He loves to hear His children <u>sing</u>, <u>worship</u>, and <u>praise</u> Him!

Shout for joy to the LORD, all the earth. Worship the LORD with gladness;
come before him with joyful songs. –Psalm 100:1-2

Additional readings: Psalm 118:24; Philippians 4:4; 1 Thessalonians 5:16

Shining stars gladly _ _ _ _, _ _ _ _ _ _ _, and _ _ _ _ _ _ the LORD with joy!

GRACE

The Lord is gracious and compassionate, slow to anger and rich in love. –Psalm 145:8

Grace is <u>undeserved</u> kindness, compassion, and forgiveness. God gives us His grace freely and expects us to be gracious (kind, compassionate, and forgiving), too. Choosing to be gracious may be difficult when someone is mean or hurtful toward us.

When someone isn't kind, it is often because he or she is hurting inside. That person may be feeling sad, lonely, troubled, confused, hurt, or frightened. When we are sensitive to a person's feelings, we begin to feel compassion, kindheartedness, and concern for that person. Then, it's easier to forgive and be gracious, even though that person hasn't earned it with his or her words or actions.

"… show mercy and compassion to one another. …'" –Zechariah 7:9

Be kind and compassionate to one another, forgiving each other, just as in Christ God forgave you.
–Ephesians 4:32

It's through God's grace that we are saved. This is truly awesome news. We'll discuss salvation in more detail on page 25.

For the grace of God has appeared that offers salvation to all people. It teaches us to say "No" to ungodliness and worldly passions, and to live self-controlled, upright and godly lives in this present age
–Titus 2:11-12

Additional readings: Colossians 4:6; Ephesians 1:6

Shining stars graciously show _ _ _ _ _ _ _ _ _ _ kindness, compassion, and forgiveness to others.

WISDOM

Get wisdom, get understanding; do not forget my words or turn away from them. –Proverbs 4:5

Wisdom is more than being smart and knowing facts. Wisdom comes from God. A wise person knows, understands, and obeys God's Word. Life is like a huge classroom. Our experiences—good, bad, fun, and sad—are all valuable lessons. The tougher the lesson, the stronger and wiser we can become. Sometimes, it is hard to understand and accept tough lessons. What we learn is our choice! We can choose to let an experience teach us negative, evil things, such as fear, hate, anger, and revenge. Or, we can choose to learn positive, good things, such as courage, love, kindness, and forgiveness. The Bible instructs us how to respond wisely to life.

Be very careful, then, how you live—not as unwise but as wise, making the most of every opportunity, because the days are evil. Therefore do not be foolish, but understand what Lord's will is.
–Ephesians 5:15-17

The days are evil means that in our everyday life, we encounter (face) things that draw us away from God and His purpose for us. Reading and memorizing God's Word in the Bible helps us to live wisely and choose God's Will for us in everything we do.

... if sinful men entice* you, do not give in to them. If they say, "Come along with us" …
do not go along with them, do not set foot on their paths … –Proverbs 1:10, 11, 15

A wise person does not let friends talk him or her into doing something wrong or evil. A wise person chooses to **TALK** with <u>God</u> when feeling pressure. A wise person will:

Think-it-through! "Is this right and true?"
Ask God for guidance and the courage to say no.
Let love rule their choice.
Keep God's Word. Follow the Bible's teachings.

If any of you lacks wisdom, you should ask God, who gives generously to all without finding fault, and it will be given to you. But when you ask, you must believe and not doubt … –James 1:5-6

Shining stars _ _ _ _ with _ _ _ when making important decisions.

*tempt, lead on, attract

PEACE

Peace I leave with you; my peace I give you. I do not give to you as the world gives. *Do not let your hearts be troubled and do not be afraid.* –John 14:27

Peace lives in our hearts and minds as happy, loving thoughts and content feelings. When we <u>trust</u> God and allow Him to be in control, we feel His calming peace. But, sometimes, we become anxious (worried) and stress about things, causing us to lose our sense of peace. God asks us to rely on Him during these tough times.

Cast all your anxiety on him because he cares for you. –1 Peter 5:7

Cast your cares on the LORD and he will sustain* you … –Psalm 55:22

At times, we don't understand or like something that happens to us and we begin to feel uneasy, restless, and confused. That's when Satan tempts us with angry, hurtful, or upsetting thoughts. When this happens to you, look at the **FACTS** before you react. Ask God and the Holy Spirit to help you:

Find ways to peacefully change what you can.
Accept the things you cannot change.
Choose wise and loving responses.
Think positively and focus on what is righteous (good, right, and true).
Study the Bible and follow its teachings.

They must turn from evil and do good; they must seek peace and pursue** it. –1 Peter 3:11

Additional Readings: Proverbs 16:7, John 14:1; 2 Thessalonians 3:16; Philippians 4:9

Shining stars _ _ _ _ _ in God instead of worrying.

*support, assist
**go after

FAITH

Faith allows us to believe that something is true, even though we cannot see, touch, hear, or fully understand it. By faith, we accept God. By faith, we are confident that His Will for us is perfect and His Word is the truth. Read: Hebrews 11:1.

God asks His children to not only have faith but to **be faithful**, too. Being faithful to God means that your heart is wholly His and you are loyal to Him. It means that you desire to do good deeds and shine for Him rather than giving in to temptation to get what you want.

What good is it, my brothers and sisters, if someone claims to have faith but has no deeds? ...
In the same way, faith by itself, if it is not accompanied by action, is dead. –James 2:14, 17

God also expects us to have faith in ourselves while working for Him. He made each of us for a special reason. His plan for us is good and perfect. We can do what seems impossible if God has asked us to do it! Remember, He often uses ordinary people to do extraordinary things so that His power can be seen more clearly.

Commit to the LORD whatever you do, and he will establish your plans. –Proverbs 16:3

Additional Readings: Matthew 19:26; Mark 9:23

When bad or sad things happen, it can be hard to keep our faith in God and in ourselves. Satan and the fallen angels work very hard to deceive and tempt us during these hard times. But, God will strengthen us and help us overcome evil attacks if we just trust Him. Faith in the truth is powerful! Faith can take away all our doubts and fears and replace them with determination and courage. When you are tempted to do wrong—be strong!

Surrender to God: *Submit yourselves, then, to God. Resist the devil, and he will flee from you.*
–James 4:7

Stand up and say: *"... Get behind me, Satan! You are a stumbling block to me; you do not have in mind the concerns of God ..."* –Matthew 16:23 (see also, Mark 8:33)

RIGHTEOUSNESS

Commit your way to the LORD; trust in him and he will do this:
He will make your righteous reward shine … –Psalm 37:5-6

God has given us the 10 commandments to live by, also referred to as THE LAW (read Exodus 20:1-17 and Deuteronomy 5:6-21 in your Bible). However, as hard as we try, we can't obey all the laws all the time—everyone will fail! Left on our own, we are unrighteous in God's eyes. The only way we can truly become righteous is through our acceptance of Jesus as our Savior. Then, the Holy Spirit will come to live in us. When the Spirit leads us, we begin to think and live righteously for God.

When asked which was the greatest commandment of THE LAW, Jesus replied:

… "'Love the Lord your God with all your heart and with all your soul and with all your mind'…
And the second is like it: 'Love your neighbor as yourself.'" –Matthew 22:37-39

It's hard to love everyone all the time—especially if a person has hurt, betrayed, or angered you. Remember to **SAIL** through those difficulties. Refer to page 16.

Additional readings: Romans 2:13; 1 John 3:7

As hard as we try, we sometimes fail to follow the Holy Spirit and sin against God and His laws. When this happens, it is very important to go to God in prayer and ask for His forgiveness. Read: 1 John 1:9.

Also, remember: to be forgiven, you must forgive others! To hold a grudge or be mean toward someone (even if you think they deserve it) is not right and goes against God's Laws.

"And when you stand praying, if you hold anything against anyone, forgive them,
so that your Father in heaven may forgive you your sins." –Mark 11:25

"For if you forgive other people when they sin against you, your heavenly Father will also forgive you.
But if you do not forgive others their sins, your Father will not forgive your sins." –Matthew 6:14-15

FRUITFULNESS

To be fruitful is to produce goodness in our lives. Fruit is a visible change in our attitudes and actions. It's an observable difference in the way we think, feel, and act. We begin to love others more freely. We find it easier to forgive. We seek to do good to everyone. We share the good news of salvation more readily. We aim to do all things for God's glory, not to make us look good to others. We pray for His continual work in us. And, so much more! To live in fruitfulness, we must <u>remain in</u> (stay connected to) Jesus.

"I am the vine; you are the branches. If you remain in me and I in you, you will bear much fruit; apart from me you can do nothing." –John 15:5

The key here is that if we don't stay connected to the vine (Jesus), we can't produce good fruit. We must remain in Jesus—follow His teachings and keep Him in our lives. He will then begin to work in and through us, so our lives will produce good fruit.

"I am the true vine, and my Father is the gardener. He cuts off every branch in me that bears no fruit, while every branch that does bear fruit he prunes so that it will be even more fruitful. –John 15:1-2

The key here is to pay attention to how you live, what you allow to influence you, what you choose to focus on, what you feed your mind with, and what you fill your heart with. Worldly desires, fame, self-centeredness, addictions, and so on often produce rotten fruit and need to be pruned (cut out of our lives).

What needs pruning in your lifestyle? What takes up too much of your time and keeps you from bearing good fruit for Jesus? It could be gaming, TV, texting, talking on the phone, an activity, a particular sport, or numerous other distractions.

Pruning also involves cutting away the bad parts of our character, so people can see Jesus' character in us. What needs pruning in your character? Are you prideful, boastful, revenge-seeking, argumentative, or selfish? Are you likely to gossip, lie, cheat, or steal?

To be more fruitful and shine brighter, ask God to prune the unproductive (unhelpful) parts of your lifestyle and your character.

Shining stars choose to _ _ _ _ _ _ _ _ Jesus, His love, and His Word.

SALVATION

For God so loved the world that he gave his one and only Son, that whoever believes in him shall not perish* but have eternal life. –John 3:16 (see also, John 6:47)

We will all die in this earthly life. Then, God will judge our lives and, unfortunately, none of us will have lived a perfect life and deserve to live forever with God. Thankfully, though, we know the good news of salvation, which is being saved from sin and its consequences, through God's gracious gift, His Son!

Everyone is promised eternal life through salvation by choosing to accept Jesus Christ and what He did for us on the cross. But, it's up to us whether we will accept or reject this gift. To accept Christ is to both believe and confess our faith in Him. It isn't enough to believe in our hearts that Christ suffered, died, and rose from the grave to defeat death and save us; we must also tell Him and others with our words and express it through our loving actions.

If you declare with your mouth, "Jesus is Lord," and believe in your heart that God raised him from the dead, you will be saved. For it is with your heart that you believe and are justified, and it is with your mouth that you profess your faith and are saved. –Romans 10:9-10

Additional Readings: Luke 11:28; Titus 3:5-6

Shining stars both _ _ _ _ _ _ _ and _ _ _ _ _ _ _ their faith in Jesus to others.

*die

BE A SHINING STAR!

Those who are wise will shine like the brightness of the heavens, and those who lead many to righteousness, like the stars for ever and ever. –Daniel 12:3

With the help of God's angels, His Word, our Savior Jesus Christ, and the Holy Spirit, you are able to do everything that God calls you to do. Part of His call is to be fruitful and lead others to Christ through your words, actions, and deeds. What you say and how you act can change someone's life for eternity. How exciting is that?!

Don't let anyone look down on you because you are young, but set an example for the believers in speech, in conduct, in love, in faith and in purity. –1 Timothy 4:12

Yes, God uses everyone, regardless of age, for His perfect purposes. Now, turn the page and have fun as you learn more about God's Word through challenging puzzles and creative activities. Your adventure into living a spiritual and fruitful life is just beginning! And, as you learn and grow in the Spirit, I urge you to ask yourself:

What special things can I do for and with the Lord that are impossible without Him?

Then, ask Him to work in and through you to accomplish those things because nothing is impossible with God!

… let your light shine before others, that they may see your good deeds and glorify your Father in heaven. –Matthew 5:16

Part Three

Activity FUN

This section may be copied for PERSONAL USE only

★ It's important to read the <u>directions</u> and the special <u>messages</u> presented on each page!

★ When coloring–be creative, use any combination of colored pencils, markers, crayons, watercolor paints, or any other materials you have.

MEMORY VERSES

1. UNSCRAMBLE the words in the left column. **2.** LOOK UP and WRITE Bible verses in the right column.
3. MATCH the right column to the correct angel in the center column. **4.** Have fun MEMORIZING each
<u>verse</u> and its <u>location</u> in the Bible. The Holy Spirit will help you. <u>Ask Him</u>!

Scramble	Angel	Verse
OJY *JOY*	Spirit	Psalm 126:3 *The Lord has done great things for us, and we are filled with joy.*
IPTSRI	Love	Proverbs 4:11
EVOL	Joy	John 15:12
CAPEE	Grace	Ephesians 4:7
SNSETGIRHUOES	Wisdom	1Corinthians 3:16
RCAEG	Peace	Psalm 34:14
USESFFUNRITL	Faith	Hebrews 11:1
STAAVLONI	Salvation	John 15:5
HATFI	Fruitfulness	Matthew 5:10
SWIMDO	Righteousness	John 3:16

28

DECODE THESE MESSAGES FROM GOD!

Write the letter for each symbol in the spaces provided
and watch GOD'S WORD appear! **You'll need to add the missing *vowels*.**

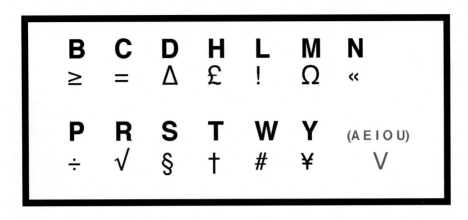

B	C	D	H	L	M	N
≥	=	Δ	£	!	Ω	«

P	R	S	T	W	Y	(A E I O U)
÷	√	§	†	#	¥	V

… ___ ___ ___ ___ ___ ;
÷v¥   vµµv«µvv«   µv   #£vµ   v   §v¥

___ ___ ___ ___ ___ ___ . —Proverbs 4:20
µvv«   ¥vv√   vv√   µv   Ω¥   #v√Δ§

___ ___ ___ ___ ___ ___ ___ ___ ,
Δv   «vµ   Ωv √v!¥   !v§µv«   µv   µ£v   #v√Δ

… ___ ___ ___ ___ . —James 1:22
Δv   #£vµ   vµ   §v¥§

We find GOD'S WORD in the ___ ___ .
£v!¥   ≥v≥!v

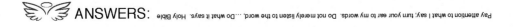
ANSWERS: Pay attention to what I say; turn your ear to my words. …Do what it says. Holy Bible

29

The Holy Spirit–

(Jesus said) *And I will ask the Father, and he will give you another advocate to help you and be with you forever–* –John 14:16

UNLOCK the combinations below using the <u>Left Right</u> chart to discover more about the Holy Spirit.
L1=A and so forth, down to **R10**=B

	Left	**R**ight
1	A	L
2	C	M
3	D	N
4	E	O
5	F	P
6	G	R
7	H	S
8	I	T
9	K	U
10	W	B

HE'S OUR:
– **L7** L4 R1 R5 L4 R6   H_____
– R8 L4 L1 L2 L7 L4 R6   _____
– L2 R4 R2 L5 R4 R6 R8 L4 R6   _____
– L2 R4 R9 R3 R7 L4 R1 R4 R6   _____
– L5 R6 L8 L4 R3 L3   _____

WHO PROVIDES:
– R9 R3 L3 L4 R6 R7 R8 L1 R3 L3 L8 R3 L6   _____
– L5 R6 R9 L8 R8 L5 R9 R1 R3 L4 R7 R7   _____
– R6 L8 L6 L7 R8 L4 R4 R9 R8 R3 L4 R7 R7   _____
– L3 L8 R7 L2 L4 R6 R3 R2 L4 R3 R8   _____
– R5 R4 L10 L4 R6   _____

Discernment is the ability to recognize right from wrong, and truth from lies. It is careful thinking. It is Biblical thinking! The Holy Spirit helps us to recognize and discern Satan's lies and deception from the truth. ASK and LISTEN. READ and LEARN.

… for Satan himself masquerades (disguises/poses) as an angel of light. –2 Corinthians 11:14

Dear friends, do not believe every spirit, but test the spirits to see whether they are from God …
–1 John 4:1

Discernment in GOD'S TRUTH is _____ _____.
R10 L8 R10 R1 L8 L2 L1 R1   R8 L7 L8 R3 L9 L8 R3 L6

**ANSWERS:** HELPER, TEACHER, COMFORTER, COUNSELOR, FRIEND, UNDERSTANDING, FRUITFULNESS, RIGHTEOUSNESS, DISCERNMENT, POWER. Biblical thinking

30

FRUIT OF THE SPIRIT

WORD SEARCH

But the fruit of the spirit is love, joy, peace, forbearance, kindness, goodness, faithfulness, gentleness and self-control. ... –Galatians 5:22-23

Find the words listed below. Look across, up, down, diagonally, and backwards.

```
G  O  O  D  N  E  S  F  R  U  I  T  S  E
A  J  S  P  I  R  I  T  P  E  E  C  E  C
S  P  E  A  C  E  H  E  L  P  E  R  L  N
N  A  K  N  G  A  D  S  H  O  L  Y  F  A
A  T  K  I  N  O  N  G  A  L  O  V  C  R
I  I  N  J  N  J  O  S  U  S  E  J  O  A
T  E  G  O  O  D  N  D  S  L  O  J  N  E
A  N  S  E  L  F  N  O  N  Y  R  O  T  B
L  C  G  E  N  T  L  E  N  E  S  S  R  R
A  E  C  E  J  P  N  O  S  I  S  E  O  O
G  E  L  F  C  O  N  T  V  S  L  S  L  F
F  A  I  T  H  F  U  L  N  E  S  S  O  B
```

GALATIANS	FORBEARANCE	SELFCONTROL
FRUIT	LOVE	JOY
PEACE	KINDNESS	SPIRIT
GOODNESS	FAITHFULNESS	GENTLENESS

Another word to describe forbearance is <u>PATIENCE</u>. Can you find it above?
<u>GOD</u> wants to be in the center of our lives. Can you find Him in this puzzle?
To produce good fruit we must stay connected to <u>JESUS</u>. Can you find Him in this puzzle?
Can you also find our <u>HELPER</u>, the <u>HOLY</u> Spirit, who helps us to grow in our spiritual fruit?

☆ Note: Some letters may be used twice.   Puzzle ANSWERS are on page 32.

LIGHT in the LORD

CROSS OUT every X, Y, and Z.
Use the remaining letters to complete God's message to YOU!

xyLzixvyxeyazszczzhxilzdyrezynxozzfzlizgxhytyaznzzdxfi
nzdxoyuytxwzhxxaytzpxzlezayyszxezszthyzeyLxoyzrzzd

For you were once darkness, but now you are light in the Lord.

_ _ _ _ _ _ _ _ _ _ _ _ _ _ _ _ _ _ _ _ _ _ ... _ _ _ _ _ _ _

_ _ _ _ _ _ _ _ _ _ _ _ _ _ _ _ _ _ _ _ _. Have nothing to do

with the fruitless deeds of darkness, but rather expose them.

–Ephesians 5:8-11

ANSWERS:

ANSWERS - FRUIT OF THE SPIRIT

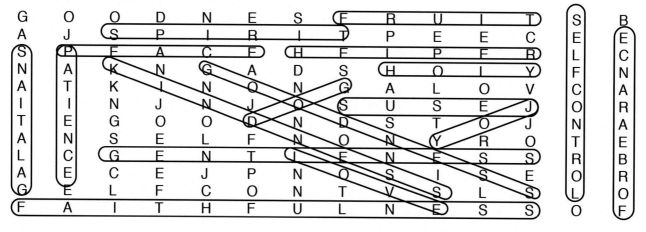

SALVATION
RIGHTEOUSNESS
FAITH
TRUTH
WORD OF GOD
GOSPEL OF PEACE

The Armor of God

Put on the full armor of God, so that you can take your stand against the devil's schemes. –Ephesians 6:11

Stand firm then, with the belt of truth buckled around your waist, with the breastplate of righteousness in place, and with your feet fitted with the readiness that comes from the gospel of peace. In addition to all this, take up the shield of faith, with which you can extinguish all the flaming arrows of the evil one. Take the helmet of salvation and the sword of the Spirit, which is the word of God. –Ephesians 6:14-17

The weapons we fight with are not the weapons of the world. On the contrary, they have divine power to demolish strongholds. –2 Corinthians 10:4

God's armor is our **spiritual defense** against the daily attacks by Satan! Our fight is against evil things that can put negative strongholds on us and pull us away from God and His perfect plan for us.

Satan's strongholds are incorrect thinking patterns based on lies, distortion, and distraction. God created us with a spirit of love and goodness. Anger, fear, hate, lying, addiction, depression, pride, and such are not from God and keep us from fulfilling His plan for our lives!

What is holding you back? Are you boastful, angry, unable to forgive someone, addicted to things like junk food or video games? These are just a few negative strongholds that keep us from shining our brightest.

MATCH the THREE COLUMNS below. 1 to 2 AND 2 to 3.

	1	2	3
a	BREASTPLATE	TRUTH	BEING MORALLY RIGHT
b	SHIELD	SALVATION	TRUST and BELIEF
c	BELT	FAITH	FACTUAL, REAL
d	SWORD	WORD OF GOD	RESCUED FROM SIN-SAVED
e	HELMET	GOSPEL OF PEACE	THE GOOD NEWS OF JESUS
f	FOOTWEAR	RIGHTEOUSNESS	THE HOLY BIBLE

God's armor may be invisible to us, but it is very real in the spiritual realm and it gives us power to stand strong against Satan's attacks. So, put God's armor on every day and be ready for battle!

Unscramble the words below found in Ephesians 6:10

Finally, be _____ (GTONRS) in the Lord and in His mighty_____(WORPE).

→ FOLLOW THE ARROWS ←

Find each **RED letter** in the Heart Chart. Then, follow the two arrows listed after it to find the <u>correct letter</u> for that number. Use the numbered letters to complete the message.

E ↑→ = **J** 1
H ↓↓ = __ 2
A ↓→ = __ 3
J →↑ = __ 4
Y ↓← = __ 5
V ←↓ = __ 6
C ↑← = __ 7
T →→ = __ 8
S →↑ = __ 9
I ↑→ = __ 10
D →↓ = __ 11
J ↑← = __ 12
L ←← = __ 13
A ↑→ = __ 14

Heart Chart

♥	T	D	L
H	Y	U	C
A →	J	O	V
E ↑¹	S	I	♥

J _ _ _ _ _ _ _ _ _ ...
1 2 3 4 3   3 5 6 7

..._ _ _ _ _ _ _ _ _ _ _ _ r _ _ _ _ _ _ _
8 9 10 2   2 5 11 12   9 13 12 2   5 3   6 12 5 10 2

_ _ _ _ _ _ _ _ • –John 15:12
8 9 10 2 7   14 9 4

ANSWERS: Jesus said..."Love each other as I have loved you.

34

LET YOUR RIGHTEOUSNESS SHINE!

GOD'S SHINING STARS are:

KIND	JOYFUL	PATIENT
WISE	FAITHFUL	GRACIOUS
LOVING	PEACEFUL	GENEROUS
GENTLE	PRAYERFUL	TRUSTWORTHY

Find the right place for each word listed above in the highlighted word below.

```
              R
              I
              G
              H
              T
              E
  S E L F — C O N T R O L L E D
              U
              S
              N
              E
    R         S
              S
```

Which of these BEST describes you?   How does it help you to help others?
Which of these do you think you need the most help with? You may want to pray about it!

Be one of God's shining STARS...

Place the letter of the correct Bible verse in front of the STARS blanks.

____ **S**ay NO to things you know are wrong.

____ **T**reat everyone the way you'd like them to treat you.

____ **A**sk and allow. Ask in prayer and allow the Holy Spirit to work through you.

____ **R**ead and remember the Bible. <u>Learn</u> and <u>obey</u> God's Word.

____ **S**eek friends who love God. Don't hang around with a bad crowd!

a. *Do to others as you would have them do to you.* –Luke 6:31

b. *Turn from evil and do good ...* –Psalm 34:14 and 1 Peter 3:11

c. *Now that you know these things, you will be blessed if you do them.* –John 13:17

d. *Do not be misled: "Bad company corrupts good character."* –1 Corinthians 15:33

e. *And pray in the Spirit on all occasions with all kinds of prayers and requests. ...* –Ephesians 6:18

√CHECK the ways you can shine for God and ~~CROSS OUT~~ the others.
Then fill in the blank below with the checked BOLD letters

- **B**elieve only the parts of the Bible you understand.
- **P**ray every day.
- **R**ead and study God's Word.
- **O**bey God's Word and His commands found in the Bible.
- **D**o whatever it takes to be popular with the in-crowd.
- **K**eep your faith a secret from those who don't follow God.
- **O**ffer forgiveness to those who have hurt you.
- **D**o to others as <u>they have done</u> to you.
- **B**end or twist God's Word to fit any situation you face.
- **A**sk God to punish those who have hurt you.
- **F**ollow the Golden Rule in all you do.

Show _____ to others that you are one of God's shining stars.

... set an example ... in speech, in conduct, in love, in faith and in purity. –1 Timothy 4:12

 ANSWERS: PROOF b, a, e, c, d

36

I AM...

1) Connect the dots–begin at 1 and end back at 1. **2)** Find the hidden message–place the letter that is next to each number in the spaces above the <u>row of numbers</u>. **3)** Write your first and last name in the center blanks. **4)** Add the missing vowels to complete star qualities. **5)** Write the special ways you can help others. **6)** Have fun coloring. When you're done, hang this in a special place!

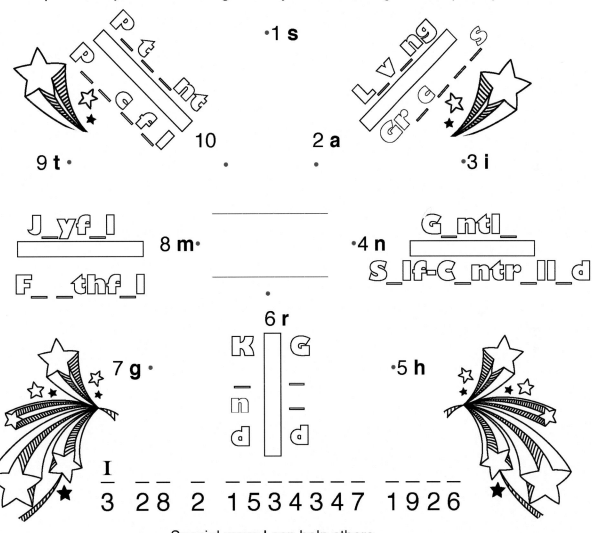

P_t__nt
P__c_f_l

•1 s

L_v__ng
Gr_c__s

10
2 a
•3 i

9 t •

J_yf_l
F__thf_l

8 m •

G_ntl_
S_lf-C_ntr_ll_d

•4 n

6 r
K   G
n   n
d   d

7 g •

•5 h

I __ __ __ __ __ __ __ __ __ __ __ __ __ __
3   2 8   2   1 5 3 4 3 4 7   1 9 2 6

Special ways I can help others…

_____

_____

37

MY JOURNAL JOURNEY

The Holy Spirit is asking you to go on a journal journey with Him!

Here's How

1. BE FAITHFUL! Same time, same place. Find a good time of day and commit to spending 20-30 minutes to journal. Pick your spot–choose a happy, quiet place to sit.

2. PRAY! Ask your helper, the Holy Spirit, to work with you to find and understand the Scriptures you need. Praise and thank Him for showing you how you can use the principles in your daily life.

3. CHOOSE A TOPIC! Anger, bullying, cheating, disrespect, envy, fear, gossiping, hate, jealousy, lying, revenge, rejection, sadness, witnessing, healing, love, joy, peace, patience, kindness, goodness, faithfulness, gentleness, self-control, and so much more.

4. BE HONEST! Search your heart for things that you are struggling with that are keeping you from shining your brightest. If you are coping with something being *done to you,* seek to find out what God's Word says about it, so you will not do the same to someone else. You are working on growing in the Holy Spirit to become the bright shining star you were created to be.

5. ORGANIZE! Make a NOTEBOOK for your journal entries. Copy opposite page or design your own.

6. BE CREATIVE! Have fun. Doodle, draw, use stickers, stamps, markers, colored pencils, or whatever.

Helpful hint* Google or ask Siri or Alexa for Scriptures on the daily or weekly topic you choose. Select two that best fit your circumstance. You can always list MORE if the Spirit moves you!

EXAMPLE

Topic: **Revenge**

My best friend Zoe is mad at Emma because Emma didn't include her in planning our team party. She won't talk to Emma and won't let her sit with us at lunch. Zoe wants me to ignore Emma, too. I'm afraid if I don't do what she wants, she'll get mad at me. I like Emma and don't want to hurt her, but I don't want to lose my best friend.

Relevant scriptures*: Ephesians 4:32; 1 Thessalonians 5:15; Matthew 7:12**

Ways to change, grow, and shine: I can remind Zoe that when I got mad at her for ruining my sketchbook, causing me to have to do all the drawing assignments over again, I forgave her. I didn't try to ruin something of hers to get even or try to get others mad at her. I can also remind her of the Golden Rule!

MY JOURNAL JOURNEY

TOPIC: _____   DATE: _____

MY THOUGHTS/FEELINGS/EXPERIENCES

_____
_____
_____
_____
_____

SCRIPTURE #1_____
_____

SCRIPTURE #2_____
_____

WAYS I CAN USE GOD'S WORD TO CHANGE, GROW, AND SHINE!

_____
_____
_____
_____
_____
_____
_____
_____
_____
_____

BOOKMARKS: 1) Copy pages using <u>card stock paper</u>. 2) Have fun coloring. 3) Cut outside the lines to create a border. OPTIONAL: Use a hole punch and add ribbon to the top.

I'm a shining STAR

Those who are wise will shine like the brightness of the heavens, and those who lead many to righteousness, like the stars for ever and ever.

Daniel 12:3

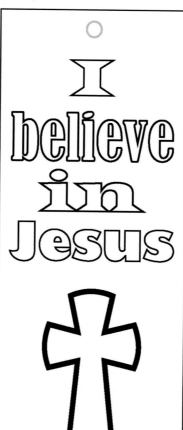

I believe in Jesus

For God so loved the world that he gave his one and only Son, that whoever believes in him shall not perish but have eternal life.

John 3:16

I'm filled with the HOLY SPIRIT

… your bodies are temples of the Holy Spirit, who is in you, whom you have received from God …

1 Corinthians 6:19

IDEA: Make multiple copies.
Write TO:___ FROM:___ on the back and give them to others.

…**Whoever lives in love lives in God, and God in them.**
1 John 4:16

Psalm 100:1

< cut on line to cut out circle

For he will command his angels concerning you to guard you in all your ways. –Psalm 91:11

Printed in the United States
By Bookmasters